PRAISE FOR

Backbone Black Bone Woman

"A love letter to Black women that pulls you close and gently coaxes you open in one piece while weaving you back together in the next. Both musing and meditation, this collection wields rhythm and breath in a way that demands witness and pause. Mesmerizing."
— Yolanda Marie

"Chioma Sheri is easy to love. She hits the right notes and soothes the tender rhythms that ache to be caressed. Her poetry is for the every days and for the fleeting moments of profound sentiments when we are lost for words. It is a sweet privilege being given a glance into the sage mind of Chioma. Thank you a million times for this blessing!"
— Dr. Alba Lamar, Artistivist, Educator, Independent Scholar

"Backbone Black Bone Woman is a harvest. It is an abundance of wisdom, celebration, and healing wrapped in verse. What must this poet have seen and lived through to cultivate these words? I am only sure of one thing, I am grateful Chioma decided to write them down." — Michael J. Ivory Jr.

Backbone Black Bone Woman

CHIOMA SHERI

Ada
PRESS
Philadelphia, PA

Cover Design by mypublishedbook.com
Interior Layout Design by mypublishedbook.com

Cover Photography/Art by Chioma Sheri

Ada Press books are available at special discounts when purchased in bulk as well as for fundraising or educational use. For details, contact the Publisher by emailing adapressbooks@gmail.com.

Printed in the United States of America.

ISBN: 9798995704324 (hardcover)
ISBN: 9798995704317 (paperback)
ISBN: 9798995704300 (ebook)

"Small but mighty."
~Grandma

Table of Contents

Introduction

There is something beautiful and whole about keeping these poems in chronological order. I think it shows the truthness of being. I think it shows the truthness of living and how the days fluctuate, how we hold on, how we let go. I think keeping it this way, makes this project archival, telling a story bigger than a single moment. Some of these poems are based on my experiences, some based on things that I've thought, things that have tarried around my mind, some based on things that I've seen, I've heard. The poems are much a part of life.

    This collection came to be before I even knew it would be –like a baby deciding that it wants to be born before even making its way into the belly. This collection, I believe, has wanted to be for as long as I've been writing or even before. I've been writing for most of my life as a way to express myself when it was hard to find other avenues, and as a way to navigate change. Poetry was and still is a power and a healing space. During Covid and the 2020 wave of the Black Lives Matter Movement, something shifted in my need for writing and creating space. It was the space born out of that time that pushed me deeper into writing and brought my friend EBJ who became my writing buddy. I found myself having writing sessions with my friend, popping into virtual spaces to write, doing multiple writing challenges (100 days haikus, 365 days of writing, writing for poetry month) many of which you will see in this collection. My poems were ritual. I wrote because I needed to, because Spirit had a word for me. My poems were a necessity, a call from and response to Spirit.

The great Audre Lorde said "poetry is not a luxury" and I've never felt that so deeply.

Within these same years, I responded to a call for submissions from a Black-owned museum. The call was for poetry by and centering Black women with a part of the "body" being the prompt/theme. I went thinking of what part of the body speaks to Black women and soon "Backbone" popped in my head. I wrote the poem which carries the title of this collection, and submitted it, but never heard anything back. And though this opportunity didn't pan out, what I didn't realize then was that this poem wasn't for the museum, it was actually for this. It was going to be the very thing that helped shape and house my poetry collection.

This collection is by no means representative of the experiences of all Black women. Nor is it my goal that this speaks to the whole story of any of our individual lives. It can't anyway because we are not monoliths. We are humans always growing and changing and experiencing new things. But it is my hope, and honestly my feeling that there is at least one poem in here that a Black woman, and quite frankly any woman, could connect to— that could speak to a part of our individual and collective stories. I was nervous at a time that the title of this book was somehow too strong or too "specific" for the poems inside of it, but I've had Black women echo my words back to me, and then I remember that I am a Black woman, and that that is surely enough.

* * *

So I invite you to journey through this collection in whatever way you'd like to move through it. I believe there is beauty in journeying, beauty in surprise, and beauty in letting a poem meet you where you are and where it is.

4/26/21
10:40pm

We sit around talking about Blackness-
One that expands beyond the borders in which we live
I ask you "How do you know so much about my mother's land?"
You say "Because Your mother's land neighbored my great great grandfather's"
I smile at how much of the world you know-
How much of the earth you've felt and carry in your backpack
I wonder how you found yourself here
I wonder why it is you so frequent my space
You say "Because You remind me of all the places I've been and loved"
On the floor,
We laugh and cross our legs
Dipping roti in egusi that you so adamantly said you must make yourself
We tell each other stories
Well into the night
Well into the morning
As if time is just ours
And the world is just us

6/1/21

I'll teach my babies about the dark
So they won't be afraid of it
So that they know they came from darkness
That before God threw light in the sky, darkness was there
They were there.
"You were there"
I'll teach you about the darkness so you won't be afraid of yourself,
So you know how to sit in it
Grapple with it
Love on it
Summon up the God who created you
And the God you came before

We'll no longer be afraid of the dark
We were told was evil
No longer afraid of the God we were told wasn't real

I'll teach my babies about the dark
So that if they're eyes are shut, then can still imagine
They can still see
So that they can create beyond what is seen in the light
That they can create in the dark
From the dark
From themselves

6/14/21
Continuum
1:43am

I've learned to be ok with "leaving"
The coming and going
The mere passing of paths
I recognize the continuum
That I must not always have the physical
That the unseen
Or the inability to touch again
Does not lessen the realness
Of what was and what is
Does not lessen my power or your power
Does not take away from the fact that
Our energy still dances on the same accord
I had to get ok with you being part of me but not part of me
You being a line in my story but not the whole of it
Not the beginning, not the end
I feel the presence of each of you
In the space between where we ended and we began

This isn't a sad poem
This isn't a prayer to go back in time
This is a recognition
A recognition
That we are timeless
That in letting go, we let live
That just like change, Spirit is constant
And we are Always
I feel you
I feel me
I thank me
I thank you

7/19/21
Undiluted

He takes his coffee Black
Says he likes it that way – straight, strong, undiluted
He takes his coffee Black
Just like he takes his women
Sippin it with ease
Says it's the only way he'll have it
It's the only way to go
He takes his coffee Black
Sitting out on his front porch
The sun resting on his skin
He's not afraid of getting darker

He takes his coffee Black
I know this cus
Im his night woman in the day
And just like his coffee
He drinks me straight
And I feel good
Cus I don't have to water down
Or sweeten up
I can just be
Me
Black as evening
And we
Can just be
Black on Black
Undiluted

8/23/21

You Poets
You Poet
You Haven – Harborer of words
You Thesaurus You
You rubbing off on me
Leaving oil stains and smells of country water
And sage
And musk
And books
And rum
And soil
You rubbing off on me
And now I'm speaking in tongues I've never spoke in
Walking in worlds that we've awoken
Even though you broken
Finished and unfinished
Whole yet still healing and
Mending with
Oil
And water
And sage
And musk
And books
And rum
And soil

9/18/21
7:22am
for grandma June

June,
The month?
June,
The poet?
June,
My grandmother
I wish I spoke to her in April
Before she left
May
Be
Maybe,
June was a woman
With a story she wanted to tell her own
I'll never know
Because
With distance and maybe ego
And maybe hurt
I let June pass me by

1/1/22

The light
The dark
Delight
I want to
delight
in it all

Journey
on the wind
greet
the sun
and the moon

To commune
with you
with God
and myself

1/5/22

It gives me so much pleasure
To know I ain't riding alone
That I ain't lonely on this trip-
On this voyage back home

I'm reminded that I'm always surrounded
Even when I feel uprooted, ungrounded

I got hands on me
Helping carry me along
I got a bag to reach into
When the journey gets long
A loving power that is holding me
When I feel far from my song

So carry on
Your well is full
Got all you need
Bountiful
Carry on Love

1/6/22

You say *"I miss you"*
I say *"I miss me too"*
I say *"I'll see you when I find myself"*
You get all misty blue

1/9/22

Everybody's leaving
      I imagine you'll be too
preparing for departure
you never told me you'd be leaving
      but I've always imagined you will-
the way your heart is always longing for a home
      I know this home isn't home enough
that these rooms get too cold sometimes
and these streets make you feel together and disjointed
all at once
      I know you'll be leaving with your backpack, your leather
      notebook, your camera, and your favorite shoes that I ain't
      pick out
you're still the closest thing to close
you've been the closest thing to close and still so far away
that's how I know
that's how I know you'll be leaving

1/14/22

It's another life
Another face
Another name
Another number
To want love these days
Is to want a dangerous thing
Arms wide open
Armed and ready to kill
To be unsafe
To be hunted
To be endangered still

To want love these days
Is to want a dangerous thing
And yet to not want it seems
As equally deadly

1/20/22

Don't want that
Don't want no half-assed love
Don't want that haphazard love
Don't want to be burning
As you watch me on fire
Don't want that
Here one day
Gone the next

I got a warmth just waiting for me
A sunlight justa beckoning my return
I got a real life love
A remember-your-name love
I got a something
At least we got a something
So I will wait
I will let go
I'll let the cold hold me for a while
Like winter held summer held fall
I'll be here
Bare and filling
Clothed and emptying
Splayed out for myself
Laid up
By myself

1/21/22

I keep imagining the house on fire
and me losing all my stuff

I imagine attempting to be ok and not
kicking myself for trying to make this
a home

I imagine me saying "i told u not to bring that stuff here" – not
your good things, not your prized things

I keep imagining the house on fire
and me losing all my stuff

I keep imagining having to create
a world all over again
while whispering to myself
"baby, you got all the stuff
you need"

1/23/22

So stuck on what I'd miss
And the things we'd never get to do
I forgot what you'd gain
I forgot that this means new possibilities–a new kind of glory for you
A better life outside this bent and broken city
This sharp and golden city
I forgot
So Ima imagine all the good things–
Your smile getting bigger
More room for you to play ball and ride your scooter
Your vision of what you believe you can be –expanding
I'll imagine those things
You aint mine anyway
You ya mama's
You ya papa's
You ya God's
You ya own

2/3/22

I can't
But you can
So let me
Do
What I can
So you can
Do
What
Only you can
Do

2/5/22

You'll get up high somewhere and leave me
because that's how it's supposed to go
that's how it's supposed to be

And I'll be here
still building this house
crossing my legs in the sun that always reaches out its
hands to touch the front of
the stoop that's ours
where we dey laugh
where we dey gist
where we dey sit

You'll only remember me
when you happen to walk this street
this street
that always has a way of talking
which means

You'll only remember me when you come home
if home is even here anymore

2/7/22
7:33am

You slapped me in the face when you said "just" a house
As if we don't live here
As if this aint where I lay my head after a long day of life-ing
As if this aint where I make my mom's special macaroni & cheese
every first Sunday
As if love making don't happen here
And I haven't shed tears here
As if this aint where we sit our asses
And toast our glasses
As if this ain't where our people gather
"Just" a house
As if what we do here ain't sacred
As if what we do here ain't enough to wanna
keep this place up
As if we ain't sacred
You think a house don't hold nothing?
You think this house can't hold nothing?
You think this magic be standing on its own?

2/20/22
a Golden Shovel after the Freedom Singers

This here woman ain't
one to be played with. Gonna
have yourself beefing with God, let
you try. This here woman ain't nobody's nobody.
She her own. She can turn
the world around with her finger - Me,
I can turn the world around.

2/24/22
Eulogy for the Living

Daughter of
Sister of
Auntie of
Mother of
She was
Beaming with sunlight
Written all over her face
Entangled all in her hair
Spirit child she was
Tryna chase after a dream
A lover
Undercover she is scattered

Son of
Brother of
Uncle of
Father of
He was
Beaming with vision
Written all over his face
Entangled all in his hair
Spirit child he was
Tryna chase after some dream
Some lover
Undercover he is weeping

They were
They are
Friends of mine

Gone but not forgotten
Gone cus they've forgotten
What the world don't want them to remember
Spirit embers

They are the living dead

3/15/22

Look, I come from holy water
holy oil
from grandma's blessings
river jordan
rosary beads
tambourine smacking
clapping
revivals after revivals
a laying of hands
a submerging into water

I come from deep songs belted into the night
6am and 9pm prayer calls

Who am I to think this rock got no power?
That I got no power simply by saying a thing is what it is and does
what it does?

I come from people who can pray a thing holy, who can sing a thing
to magic, and a God who spoke a world into existence

3/20/22
Around 3:56pm

Things fall apart
Then fall together
Falling in love with you again
You city
You world of a woman

4/4/22
Don't Be Sad Girl

Don't be sad girl
That ain't nobody singing bout you
And ain't nobody writing bout you
And ain't nobody rushing to sketch your face
Or take your picture
Don't be sad girl
Don't you know
The Ancestors been crooning your name
Grandmothers been praying for you
The Universe been waiting for you
You been on God's tongue and mind
Since the beginning of time
Don't be sad girl, Woman
Cus you special

4/15/22

I can't take another Black death
-
You can't take another Black life

4/17/22

Remembering
Everything that I used to love
Seeing you now jogs my memory
Undoing the distance of this underground
Railroad I traveled to survive
Remember when we were young?
Earth was more than a thing to be buried under,
remember?
Crafting stories? Counting stars?
Thinking wildly?
I remember
Oppressed.
Never dead. This is our time.

4/23/22

I keep finding home
Home keeps finding me

4/27/22

Late night poetry
Whispering sweet things in ears
Late night music
Dancing with no care
In the world of who's watching
Who's got something to say
About how we survive?

5/8/22

Mother was home
Before this house was
Flesh and blood were teachers
Mother was home
Much after dark
This house, it held her features
I played in her room
Like I swirled in her womb
Trying on her shoes and wigs
The mother I never knew

Was always working
Just to care for us her kids

5/11/22
Foreign Bodies
Free write with ebj

Native,
Native
You felt native to my mind
Yet foreign to my body
What ship did you travel on to get here
What were you trying to conquer
Let's go back
Can we go back
Can you go back
To the land you know
To the land I've known of you
You parted me
Sectioned me up
Colonized my legs, my feet, my breast
And you named them
Names I do not know
Names I'm still trying to learn
I'm no longer a native speaker in my own home
My own body

5/14/22
a haiku

Black baby blues are
Indigo - deep color soft
Like sapphire sky

5/16/22

Nothing makes sense without you
Dark matter
They still don't know what you're made of

5/20/22

We've been finding our way
Back to each other
Big me, Little me
Like you needed me back then
Like I need you right now

6/23/22

We're two parts of the same world
Split in half by an equator
When you're in light
I'm in dark
When you're in dark
I'm in light
I went chasing after you
Was I too afraid to sit with myself?

Running from me was
Running from you
Running from you
Was running from me

Could never catch up
Running in circles
Not resting in the fact that
We're two parts of the same world
Could never catch up cus I wasn't supposed to
Light warrior
Shadow warrior
Both needed
Cyclical
Two parts of the same coin
Two parts of the same world
This joy
This grief
Same world
Same world
Two parts two parts
Two part love
Two parts love

6/25/22

It always ends like this
I the loser?
Winner?
Were we playing games?
Were you playing nice?
Going easy on a sistah
Until she wears herself out
It always ends like this
I the loser?
Winner?

7/5/22

I pray you, I pray me
Working hand in hand, I pray free
I pray us, I pray we
I pray open eyes, I pray see

You I pray, me I pray
Hand in hand working, free I pray
Us I pray, we I pray
Open eyes I pray, see I pray

7/7/22

This ending is another beginning
We beginning again–
What has always been but differently
Like home – we beginning again
Like love – we beginning again
Like friendship – we beginning again
We begin when we end
We start when we finish–
A chapter, a season
Again
We beginning again

What ended was once a beginning
So why you so afraid to let go?
Afraid of transition?
Afraid to begin again?
You think this life ain't cyclical?
You think when something dies,
Another thing ain't born?
Given space to grow?
It's beginning
You beginning
You beginning again

7/16/22

Soledad,
You named me.

Was I destined to be alone
Or a deity?
The irony
As I speak my name
In the quiet
To a loud earth that doesn't hear me

Soledad.

Did you foreshadow
This - the mark of my existence -
Carrying lonely or did you think me holy?
Carrying some savior, a revolution
That could only be birthed here
In my

Soledad?

7/18/22

I gotta read poems
From a far away somebody
From a dead and gone somebody
So I don't fall in love with
A close thing
A living thing
Except the living word
Not bone and marrow
Breathing breath
Beating chest or
Dancing flesh

Gotta read poems
From a far away somebody

8/6/22

You're full of stories
I can't see them in your face
But I see them in the way you curl your hands
To take a picture
The way you touch with question
And sit back with answers
I see stories in the way you hide your stomach
And on the days you let it show
In the way you eat slow
And greedily sometimes
The way you walk away from me when things get uncomfortable
Stories
Written in the ways you do
Stories
Written in the ways you don't

Stories and stories
I read
I make up
Are they made up of truths?
Are they made-up
Prettier than they are?
Uglier than they are?
Are we made up?
I thought you real
But are you made up?

8/12/22

I used to think we were different
Couldn't hear past the noise
Of my own insecurities
Thought cus you wear your hair up
And I wear mine down,
That we both ain't cry in the morning
That our hearts didn't break the same
That you didn't know or want to know my name
But
I see you now
Your hair up and my hair down
We talking to each other
With our mouths
With our eyes
Saying
"I see you"
"I been you"
"I am you"

Used to think we were different
But deep down
We been the same
Just journeying in different lanes
Crossing each other

Please forgive me

8/15/22

Then there was
sweet honey in the rock

Something soft
amidst something hard

Something tender
amidst something tough

Something singing in the quiet

Holding me
Rocking me

Solid enough to stand on
Soft enough to rest in

There's always
Sweet Honey in the Rock[1]

---

[1]   In homage to "I Be Your Water" by Sweet Honey in the Rock

8/17/22

Hungry for something
not filling
not feeling me

How do you satisfy
the not wanting wants
of fried things
and greasy lovers
who slip out of sight
time and time again

How do you satisfy a craving
that scathes you?

8/23/22

Tabs and tabs open. *Click*, there's more. Files and files on screen, keep adding up. More and more weight on my head means more and more weight on my back, my shoulders. My legs can't hold this upper body. Feet **ache**, feels **broken**, can't move. Forgetting to breathe, to stretch, to eat, to sleep. Forgetting? No time to? **Too tired** to eat, to stand to cook a meal, **too numb** to feel the sun outside, this light on my skin, this love barging in. **Too tired** to think of what to eat, **too tired** to pay attention to where and how I sleep. On sofa, sure I'm messing up my spine. They laid off six of us today. Us as in skinfolk. **Talks** and **talks** and **talks**, not addressing the reality of race, another smack in the face. **Another tab** and **tab**. **Bills**, bills, evidently we cost too much to keep, tabs and tabs and tabs, that's hard for me to close, accruing, accruing. Tired. *Who's left to pay for all this?*

8/30/22

I want to go where the jazz is playing
Where the trumpets blowing
Where the brothas going hard on the keys
Where the drummer don't miss a beat
And the sistas don't miss a step
I want to go where the jazz is playing
Cus I've had enough blues

8/30/22

I'm where the jazz is.

9/8/22

Beyond this country
There are places
Where rest isn't only on weekends
Where laughter meets you religiously
And the sun kisses you like a lover
Where little is a lot
Play comes easy
And joy comes not only in the morning
But in the midday and night
Beyond this country
There are
Other ways of doing
Of living
Of being
Beyond this country
There are other worlds

9/15/22

Tell me of the world you see
Not sure my
Eyes will get to see it all
But don't feel sorry for me
My eyes have seen a
World of you
A world in this here
Town
A world in my here
Life
So don't feel sorry for me
Just, tell me of the
World you see

9/18/22

You, other man
You lover man
You smile
So big
Sweet
You hug so tight
Heat
Sweat
Drifting
To God knows where
Bet
Far from here
Bet
You other man
Lover man
Drifting

9/27/22

Tired though I slept
Thirsty though I drank
Walking though I fell
Swimming though I sank

9/29/22

Do you like to be sad
Because it brings you poetry?
Do you like to be sad
Because it makes your waters deep?
Do you like to be sad
Because it makes you a better blues man
Gives you something to sing and write about?
So the world can finally listen to you
Cus they seem to like you blue
Like a Black man can't be any other color
Just Blue man
Skin
Just Blue man
Song
Just Blue man
Love
Just Blue man
Dream

Do you love or hate
Or
Do you love and hate
This
    Your
Sad ass
Pretty ass blues?

10/8/22
for grandma Priscilla

You didn't got to college
Cus that was men folk's business
But you went to school
On the farm
In the house
At the church
In the factory
On your walks to and from the stream
You're a stream of
Wisdom
Grace
Power
Knowledge
No you didn't go to college
And you didn't have to

10/9/22

I feared leaning in
Cus
I feared falling
Cus
I feared hitting ground hard
Cus
I feared breaking
Cus
I feared not being able to put back together
Cus
I felt
Insecure/unsecure

10/11/22

Always feel like
I'm pulling
Having to pull teeth
Pulling
Having to pull hairs
Pulling
Having to pull it together
Pull
Pull
Tug; it's war
Pull
Pull
It's mine; it's yours

Pulling

10/13/22

I'm a storyteller
But not a storyteller
Though sometimes I tell stories
And make believe

And do believe

That they're real
That if not mine
They're somebody's
That if not yours
They're somebody's
And if not ours
They can be
Story
Telling truths
Stories
Telling real
Stories
We feel

10/14/22
9:55pm
in memory of Ms. Joilet & those who've journeyed on

We rise in glory
We fall in glory
We down
We up
A thousand thousand stories
Will be told
Because we lived
Will be lived
Because we told
The world we're here

With a fist raised up
Or a head held high
With hands upon our hips
Or hair reaching the sky

With songs so sweet
Or a crooning so deep
With a praise so loud
Or a stomping of our feet

We rise in glory
We fall in glory
We down
We up
A thousand thousand stories
Will be told
Because we live
We live
Oh, we live

10/18/22

You remember me
When I've forgotten myself
You
Hear me
When I can only halfway speak
Tongue tied and tired
You see me in the dark
And in the light
When I fright
Fight and fleeting
You feel me in my tender
In my hard
Loud and laughing
You, me
You me

10/20/22

I got a lot of earth in me....

10/24/22

My savior
Was my feet
Didn't know it
Until it touched the water
I waited
Until I waded

10/25/22

Don't know where she's been but
I can tell she's been a lot of places
There's journey in her face
Feel "been to" in her embrace
Hear "been through" in her voice
I see no better choice
Than to take my time with her

Give her rest from all her travels

11/1/22

This poem needs morning
Needs tomorrow
Needs full day
Nothing on your plate
Needs time
Kneading
This poem needs rest
To rise

This poem needs a
Sunday
Needs a Saturday
Needs a Sabbath
Needs a God

It's dust
And it's breath
It's spirt
It's flesh

This poem needs more than a minute
Needs more than I can give it
Tonight
This poem needs morning

11/2/22
Prompt: "If you fill your mouth with a razor, you will spit blood"
~ African Proverb

the Aftermath
is cleaning
a whole lot of scrubbing
hydrogen peroxide
bleach
the Aftermath
is questionings
getting woke up in my sleep
by the babies
or the nightmares
or your nightshakes
you'll smile and say
"baby, you don't have to eat what I eat"
or
"baby, I don't bring none of that in the house"
or
"baby, I know how to handle my stuff"
or
"baby, I'm fine and you fineeeeeee"
the Aftermath
is sweet-talking
backbreaking
poetic and uneasy

don't know exactly what you eating
but it's eating you quickly
eating me slowly
killing us softly

11/4/22

I wanna *hang*
As in these clothes up I'm wearing
Last year's dress
That the lover who left me left me
Twenty year-old tights
Still hoisted up to my chest
Cus I don't wanna be touched
But I wanna be touched
I wanna hang
And I wanna hang
With you

11/5/22
a haiku

We heal untethered
And tethered, holding on and
Letting go, we heal

11/10/22

Enwere m ụlọ
Here and there
I have a home
Because your arms welcome me
As if I never left
As if I've always been
As if I'll always be
Daughter
Sister
Enyi
Ulo
Enwere m ụlọ

11/25/22

New kid on the block
You grew up on
Things feel so new
Old things
You never knew
Legs wobbling
Why can't you stand?
No one to hold your hand
You been here before
But you ain't never been here before
This you
With a full set of teeth
With a mouth full of song
With a body that's known sometime love
You ain't been here before
But you've been here before
With a head full of dreams
With a heart full of love
And a journal full of story
So walk
You can walk
With what you remember
Holding on to what you don't know
But feels steady
Steady

11/29/22

hands
you lend me
hands
you give me your
hands
I can hold
hands
me something sweet
hands be something rough
hands be something story hands
be

12/5/22
Mini Male Order Catalog
inspired by Wanda Coleman's "Male Order Catalog"

Bedstuy till I die, prettier than I like em,
afro, fitted jeans, denim jacket, marvin gaye
listening, had me sick and stupid. Thought it
sweet to tell me of other lovers.

Florida water, tall drink of water, always on the
water, wit to match mine, slick, could never
catch a hold of him, high-top, made in Haiti,
Said "dont let nobody play you." Wanted more
of my body than it could give.

Small thing, flannel shirt, loved Jesus, hated
nigeria and what felt like himself, spoke malay
but never forgot his pidgin, them say "yahoo
boy," kind. Married within a year of our
departure.

12/11/22
Duplex (Who Will Be My Friend This Time?)

Back at it again, at it again
Will it be my friend this time?

      Will this time let you be my friend
      Or will it make us hate each other?

The mind makes us hate each other
I remember the last proposal

      The last proposal - pretty, went sour
      I can still taste it on my tongue

I still want to taste you on my tongue
They say don't eat when you're already full

      I'm already full of poetry
      This proposal got me at it again

Back at it again, at it again
Will I be my friend this time?

12/19/22
1:08pm

This all new to me
I knew old almost—
Touched its hem
But it didn't heal me
Hemmed in
By ragged edges
Could never touch the whole
Could never want me whole
This old.....

This new
I wanna know
Is this new, old?
Decrepit?
Just as broken
Or can I touch the whole ?
Can it want me whole?

12/27/22
4:30am

Gone gone
And dusted
Busted
I dream free
I dream bondage
Roped at the neck
By the words of the people
By the quiet of my love
Screaming "GET ME FREE!"
Screaming "GET ME FREE!"
But we both tied up
With work, with hurt, with tired
Of what he said/she said/they're doing
Why they ain't here no more?
Where did daddy go?
Where did mommy go?
What side they on
On the auction block
The other side of heaven?
I hope they free

Who will get us free ?
How will we get us free ?
I dream freedom
I dream bondage
Scared up out my sleep
What's real anymore?

"Can you see me? Is that you?"

12/29/22

My shoulders cry
a country on my back

1/1/2023
8:40am

I'm sure she loved
And she loves
And she love

1/23/23
from journal 7:11am

You love me, and hate my poetry
He hates me, and loves my poetry
Who will kill me first
When the word is me?
Who will kill me first
When I am the word?
Or did I enlist to die myself?
To dine myself
With lovers who will turn me over
For a piece of silver
And a chance at fame?
Who will remember me sometimes
Then forget my name
Who love me partially

Until the poetry is sweet enough
Or the outside's too bitter

2/3/23
9:40pm

Baby
You just need to break
Open
Yoke
This won't be over easy

2/19/23
Backbone Black Bone Woman

this house of a nation
would fall
without you
this home of a woman
would break

back
bone

like our grandmothers

when i am lost
i go
back home
backbone
Black
Bone
Woman

when we are lost
we go
back home
backbone
Black
Bone
Women

3/1/23
9:36pm

don't you see this flesh?
bending towards you
wrapping around you
around you
telling you
your dreams ain't ghosts
and you ain't figment

you're real
enough to touch
enough to see
enough to be

dont you see aaaaalll this flesh?
welcoming you
right
where you are?

3/2/23
3:24pm

I feel it
Up and down my bones
Rummaging through marrow

Like my people

When it eats, it leaves nothing

/anxiety/

3/22/23
12:05am

Will you let me go
Or your
Ego

5/19/23

He talked me to death
And I listened
Went following his word to my own crucifixion
He talked me to death
Talked my ear off, my arm off
Talked and talked
Until I was pieces
Until I was just foot and hand
Until I was just finger and toe
Until I was just nail - chipping
And chipping
He talked me to death
Till I couldn't find me no more
Till I couldn't see me no more
He talked me out of existence
Until the only story, I could repeat back
Was his
Until the only truth I knew
Was that which he told me
He talked me to death

Then she- Black Woman
Sister, friend, auntie, mother, lover, grandmother, spirit
Spoke me to life
Raised me from my dead
With a word
With a song
With a gospel
Like she been there before
Like she been here before

She spoke me to life
Like she knew me
Like she saw me
And loves me for who I am
She spoke me to life
Piecing me back together

Molding me whole
With her stories, my stories,
She spoke me into existence
Till I could see myself again
Until the stories I could repeat back was ours
And the truth I knew was mine
She, they, like God spoke me to life

5/23/23
6:48am

Who gives grace
To the Black girl with no face
To the Black girl with soft lips
To the Black girl with closed hips
Who gives grace
To the hand that feeds them

6/4/23
4:05am

Every third weekend of the month
He goes
To his other woman's house
They play house like we do
Then he leaves
Does she fall?

She keeps the home
Just as I keep the home

I envy how he can travel
And always have a home
A place he can forget then return
To be welcomed like the prodigal son

I figure I need to make this place a resting station— a safe
spot for my sista
So she too
Can come and forget
When she travels
If she travels
a prodigal daughter

6/8/23
11:08am

There are things we know
Before they happen
That we'll get eaten
Before the bite
Before the mouth opens
Before the eyes look our way
There are things we know
Before they happen
The manner in which
We'll be devoured
How there
Will be no gratitude
For nourishing

We as women
Know these things
Before they happen

6/13/23
6:59am

I think I need
Your hands around
My waist your tongue inside
This face of mine
I think i need
A trembling night
Between my thighs

what I think
what I know

I just need a touching
From some
Body

A hug from somebody?

9/4/23
8:26am

My words-
They went
Back to the river which they came
Can't hear them but don't you feel them
Flowing?
Rushing towards something
An ocean? A belly of a child?
A woman, a me
- thirstier than they've ever been
From pouring and pouring
You can bear the fall, but
Can you bear the rise?
The tide, the breath,
The breadth?
     My words
     My words
     Went back to
The river which they came

1/1/24
9:19pm

i want to unfold in hands
that know prayer
that know give without take
that finds rest in the caressing
of scalp
in journeying
the bend of an eyebrow
curve of an ear
mountain of a nose
expanse of a cheek
the holy
of my face
i want to unfold in hands
that know
hands that care
hands with enough room

1/3/24

Rhythmic it feels
Dancing
           boppin
In my non existent heels
It heals
to have your own beat
Warmed by your own heat
The tapping of my own feet

1/14/24
4:30pm

She's tired
Too tired to longer speak the language I know-
My first, my only
Her second
Every second she leans deeper
And deeper into what came first-first tongue
First, second, I wonder the last time she's been touched
By anyone but God
She's tired
Too tired to longer speak the language I know
So I hear whatever the wind tells me
To place my hand on her skin
When's the last time she's been held
By anything but a bed?
Hospital beds
Can they feel the weight of all the things
She's held
Up?
Together?
The children—hers and the ones left for dead
The homes almost breaking
Marriages, families aching
And oh the babies…..hers and the grands and the great grands…
She's tired
Too tired to speak the language I know
I know
I know
She's been
Tired

1/16/24
5:26pm

She asks the hard questions:
"What do you see in the future?"
I answer:
I can't see past the edge of my bed
"Well what do you see at the edge of your bed?"
I'm annoyed
And then startled by the fact that there are things there:
A journal I can't seem to write in
A book I've been wanting to read
A teddy bear I struggle to hold
A wallet full of credit cards im never late on paying
A possibility I'm afraid is not possible
And suddenly I see it
I see it
A world
Right at the edge of my bed
A poem
To my surprise
In reach
I reach

What has she done?
How did she do it?

She asks the hard questions

1/20/24

On and up, on and up. Let us get on and up. We got this God thing – good thing, made in the image of the Supreme, image of the greatest God, image of the universe. On and up, on and up. Let us get on an up. All you need is all you have, now what you gonna do with it? What you gonna do with it? Do with it, be with it, life with it –magic, magic, magic spellbinding magic –Do magic, Be magic. Be, be, be, you got all you need. Speak like you write – the voice is here. The words are here –the vision been here –Been here – been here. Lean into this unknowing that already knows, this unknown, that already knew. Lean in, lean in. You got it. God got you. And baby you Got God! Got God in yourself!

4/1/24
a haiku

Calling in the deep
Deep. She says she wants nuthin
Nuthin but my feet

4/2/24

this body carries wells
carries wails
carries wails
of a thousand mothers
this body carries jubilation
cantations
songs of a far away place
of a long ago time
this body carries wells
carries wails
this body carries well
until it doesn't
until it swells
until it breaks bone
until it's back breaks
then out comes a flooding
in the lungs
brimming in the eyes
a tear?

this body
this body carries well
carries wells
carries wails

4/3/24
9:27pm

I am my mother's daughter
She is her mother's daughter
We all stubborn
Rock
All a little crazy

I'm not like them tho
I say
I think
I catch them
In the mirror sometimes
Looking back at me
Looking back at me–
A history

4/9/24
7:10am

Heathen
But heaven sent me
Called me out by my name

I came
Running out the gates
Dressed in darkness
Shining in light

They
Dazzled by my night
Star struck
Covered their
Eyes
Wide open

Heathen

Made the blind folk see
Even when they aint wanna

Heathen
Sounds so close to heaven

4/17/24
11:25pm

This lady | woman knows God
Says death is another life
She's been here before

4/23/24
1:55pm

today i take | took a breath
feels like i been tryna catch it
for over a decade
kept missing it
holding it
seem to never find
the right time or the place
as if breathing aint a birthright
what it birthed right here in front of me
i feel born again
hopeful
God

4/24/24
8:42pm

I tell stress
To have a seat
I let breath
Take my hand
Be my man
My woman
For the night
Let em dictate my step
As stress watches
With lips curled up
And rolling eyes
Thought they had me
For the night
But it's me and breath
Sliding and gliding
Into each other
Turning the heads of everybody
A Black woman and her breath
Is a wild thing to some | see

4/25/24
4:10pm

period pains
gut wrenching
turns my body into a thing
that eats itself
disobeys all orders
try to stand up
yanks me down
attempt to go out the door
turns me around
makes me remember

the downside of being alone

somewhere inside of me
it manages to grow
just enough of an arm to
get me to a tylenol or a text
enough of a leg to
carry me to a toilet or a bag
to convulse before it slithers back
back into a thing
i'm familiar with
it's a beast
that pick and chooses
how it comes

4/26/24
10:18pm
Blackout poem after Zora Neale Hurston's
Their Eyes Were Watching God

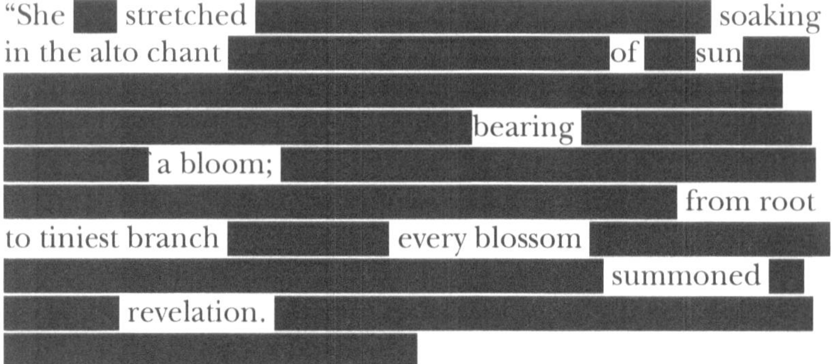

4/30/24
8:24am
a Golden Shovel after Lucille Clifton

i inhale it
even as hard as it is
to take in the
air of life
a living thing
even in
the in-between of us
suffocating, that
relentless breath - a will
i did not
write, to let
the exhale meet us
bringing life to what seemed left to die

8/6/24
7:08pm
Written in Marquita's TNT Write Nights
Prompt: "The cup is full - a student & teacher's last lesson or parting."

Parting my hair in sections
Ready, not ready to interlock this moment

Cutting my hair again,
Another round of shedding

Should I write how much I miss her?
We've always spoken in art
I want her to see who she's helped me
Become

Braver Now.

I enter the room and she sees me
She enters the room and I see her

Our final lesson together on "seeing"
Our final lesson together on "being seen"

Oh, how I wish we could begin again
Oh how we know, we're already
Beginning again

8/10/24
7:47am on my walk
for the woman on 45th Street

She tends her garden still
As her home crumbles
Developers - don't care about foundations
Don't care what breaks
When they build

YOU MUST GO
She stays
YOU MUST LEAVE
She prays
She paves a way of resistance

Can't pay her out her own
Can't push her out her home
Bulldozers can't knock this one down

Still pouring water on what's left
Such a pretty sight
To an ugly fight

She tends her garden still
Cus She knows that something remains
Even if that something
Is simply a Black girl who walks by and notices

8/12/24
8:45pm

First:	we survive
You wake	with ritual
Lift your head to the sky	
Second: pour out a heap of praise	coming together and remembering
This is the day that the Lord has made	that we are making
Next you pray	so we don't forget
2 cups gratitude	grandma's recipe
3 cups petitions	faith without works is dead
7 tablespoons in Jesus Name	
	we survive
	with ritual

9/12/24
Reaching (poem & song)[2]
First stanza written in 2019

I found myself reaching
I found myself reaching
For something outside
Of myself
As if the heavens weren't in me
As if the stars weren't in my eyes
The clouds in my breath
Home in my belly
I found myself
I found myself
Reaching

Rummaging through
20 year old memories
For a sweet girl
With a loud voice
And louder dream
Looking for the pieces I thought fell off
When heavy hands fell on
This body of mine

Went searching for
This body of mine
This being of mine

I found myself reaching
For something outside of myself
Rummaging through old piles of clothes
Old piles of men, of lovers
Of back handed compliments
And let me downs
And closed doors

---

[2]   This poem was created for and initially performed as a collaborative piece with singer and musician Leah Wrenne.

Rummaging through doubt
And doubt
And doubt
Cus I'm just Black
And I'm just simple
And I'm just an ordinary woman

These days I've been
Coming to myself
Simply coming to myself
Running to myself
Swifty running to myself

Seeing the home
Right here in this lush flesh of mine
Making a pillow of these shoulders
So I can rest
Rest assured

That I'm all right here
I'm alright here

Remembering instead of dismembering
This body of mine
This being of mine

Beeeeen time to bear witness
To the fruit of myself
The juice of myself
My own sweetness

It's all right here. It's alright here.

Just an ordinary woman,
An extraordinary women
Reaching
Reaching
Inside of myself

11/2/24
3:21pm (naija)

no longer waiting
to be met how I meet

I meet myself every morning
round 4 or 5
with how you feeling love?
I let myself open to myself
and my God
We perform a living poetry
and if I weep (and some days I do)
We meet me with arms
and when my words come rushing
in ways that seem to make no sense
We say they have meaning
and if there are no words at all
We say "I hear you."

I don't save softness for tomorrow
softness to when I feel i'm broken enough
or softness till when someone feels I deserve it

I don't save softness for everybody but me.
no, I meet me how I meet the world,
how I meet the ones I love
every morning, every evening, every afternoon
every damn time I almost catch myself waiting

11/14/24
6:30am (naija) - 11/15/24 (us)

there's story in your bones
a eulogy in your sweat
for all the things you've had to tarry over
this walk, i've seen before
this flesh i've known…
how you carry the sway
of many the men i've loved
a softness etched out of hard tradition
breaking free, a desire (so close and far in reach)
heavy feet
with some kind of levity

i see you
as you pass on by like a song
and i, in my sweet nostalgia, sing along

2/25/25[3]

you feel like a thousand islands
dressing me with your hands
addressing me by my name
we feel like a thousand islands
touching each other
or maybe a country—newly freed
renaming itself
we feel like Burkina Faso - 1984
reclaiming itself
an old and new religion- boldy
proclaiming itself
historically oppressed tongue and body – art
reframing itself

we just tryna love…
like a country that's never been colonized
tryna love back– precolonial
tryna love Black - forward - beyond the future

tryna love now
you and I - a thousand islands
dressing us with our hands
addressing us by our names
we
just tryna Love
we
just tryna Love
we
just tryna Love

We
Just
Tryna
Love

---

[3]   This piece was originally completed (in its old rendition) on 12/25/22. It was revamped on
       2/25/25 to the poem you see now.

2/15/25
Remember Me Today
5:14pm

Remember me tomorrow
Remember me today
Remember so you don't forget
We are the truth, the way

Practice what I taught you
Recipes, prayers, songs
Remember that these rituals
Will help you carry on

Speak the words of Octavia
Audre, Grandma, and the Psalms
In times of tribulation
These too will be a balm

On days that you grow weary
Don't forget to rest
Know that there's a way we've paved
So you can take a breath

When there looks to be no way
And all you see is pain
Practice letting go and grieving
Then shine your eyes again

Know that change is constant
And you are changing too
The past, present, and future
Is all inside of you

Black is the beginning
Black will be the end
The darkness is a birthing place
It's where you find the light my friend

Remember how I always said
Charity begins at home?
Well Home is all the meat of you
Your spirit, mind and bone

So Speak this back tomorrow
And Speak this back today
Speak this till your being knows
You're sunshine and clay

Fri. Dec 2, 2022

PREPARED BY

DATE 12 | 2 | 22

[Exercise #1: The Word]

Flower

~~The~~ Figuring out how to
How do I plant myself in my own sacrity
With honor and respect when my stem has been crushed
When my flower hasn't bloomed
                recognizing the curves in   of me
~~How do I~~ ~~recognize~~ the ~~fingerprint~~ in the garden ~~that I am~~
When you say these flowers, my flowers are out of season

Tethered

I remember the day I told myself I could no longer be tethered to
the grief of losing myself
I couldn't move, I couldn't breathe
Because I realized that I never mourned the metamorphosis that I am
I simply burned her dead parts away

December

Bundled in December ... in your arms ... in your embrace
Before I used to hate winter because being cold alone is no fun
But you, my beautiful December baby, you are the memories of
snow angles that taught me to appreciate the cold ⌐
To not worry about how much I looked forward to ⌐
                                                   to greet the
But   sharp winds that cut
I'm learning to water myself
With grace, honor, safety b/c I am sacred water   at the gray spaces
                                                   in between
So I grow
I bloom   To exist in a place that
                      is always the first   I don't have to dread Dec
Flower   and last   ← because discovering you + us

---

[1] Scanned copy of poems written by my dear friend Brandie, in a workshop I held. These poems were written freewrite and later returned to. Brandie will always be a poet. And she was always a supporter of me and my work. *Thank you Brandie. You are missed and remembered.* <3

12/2/22[5]
Flower
By Brandie Marie McCoy

Figuring out how to plant myself in my own holy devotion
With honor and respect when my stem has been crushed
When my flower hasn't bloomed
Recognizing the curves in the fingerprint in the garden of me
When you say these flowers, my flowers are out of season
But I'm learning to water myself
With grace, honor and safety...because I am sacred water
So I grow
I bloom
Flower

---

[5]   Brandie's poem in completion - as she shared it with me. Written to the word "flower."

Acknowledgments

By Chioma Sheri
my sister friends across state lines,
we all have a seat at the table, 2024

Where do I begin to begin?

Thank you God. Thank you Spirit. For always speaking to me and being present through it all.

Thank you reader for journeying with me and staying the journey. This work continues to breathe because of you.

To EBJ, my friend, I am not certain this collection would exist in the way it is without you–our endless nights of chatting and writing together. Thank you for believing in my poetry and for being one of the people I was always excited to share my poems with.

To Khalisah Hameed from The Olive Press Media, thank you for giving my baby her first developmental edit read. It was the guide I needed.

To Vanessa | Vespera, thank you for being this collection's sacred doula- giving my baby her close and final edits. You saw me, my work, and the spirit of my work in ways language can't articulate. Thanks for helping me birth her with authenticity and clarity.

To Tracy Chiles McGhee, thank you so much for your patience and guidance in helping me format and publish this piece. Your tender assistance made this process lighter.

To Al McCoy, thank you for being my friend and a brilliant poetic mind. You've beared witness to my "truthness" while offering your creative thought and fierce edits to some of these pieces. Thank you for believing in my spirit. And thank you immensely for giving me the permission to let Brandie's words close out and live on in this collection. Beyond grateful.

To my sistafriends, all of you. Special shout out to my "Black yoga sistafriends" (you know who you are) especially Sherrell and Yolanda Marie for the way you saw and loved up on my poetry, Kelly for speaking a WORD to me that one night at my place that opened something up in me and reminded me I need not contort my work to fit into any kind of box, and Sharon for joining me on poetry challenges, that inspired me and helped keep me writing.

And to so many more of you, named here and named in my heart. Please know that I am forever grateful.

To my 8th grade English teacher Ms Marine who told me to keep writing, thank you. To Ms Patrice for leaving comments on my poetry posts that would create a river in me, thank you. To Chris for your pep talks, to Nüma for all the ways you remind me of the beauty of my words, to all my friends here and afar, thank you.

To my family. Special shout out to my siblings, aunties, little cousins, nieces and nephews. Thank you. Love you so.

And thank you to the women who came before me - my grammy, my mommy (I love you) and the women who came with me - my dear sister, and all my sisterfriends.

It is your living that has made for mine and the energy of your collective lives that made me know that this book

deserves to be. Thank you for being. Thank you for living.

Author's Notes

"Undiluted" *was originally published by Brittle Paper in 2021*

"11/2/22" *was originally featured on the AFIA podcast in 2022*

"Don't be Sad Girl" *was originally published in "Finding Paradise: A Black Mental Health Anthology" in 2022*

"Remember Me Today" *was originally published by Love Now Media in 2025*

About the Author

Chioma Sheri is a Philly native of Nigerian and Jamaican descent who has a hate-like relationship with writing bios. She has a background in African American Studies and deeply believes in the power of storytelling and community memory-keeping, specifically with regard to how we hold and support stories from Africa and the diaspora. A Listener, Holder of space, Lover of God and People - She's a sometimes Poet, sometimes Performer, all times Learner, Storyteller, and Bearer of Laughs. You can find her cooking, researching, spending time with the people she loves, cracking herself up, and co-hosting book clubs & writing circles.

9 7 9 8 9 9 9 5 7 0 4 3 1 7